THE POETRY PAD

Sue Thomas

**Missouri Center
for the Book**

🐸🐸🐸

Missouri Authors
Collection

Royal Fireworks Press

Unionville, New York
Toronto, Ontario

ABOUT THE AUTHOR

Sue Thomas graduated from the University of Northern Iowa with a Bachelor of Arts Degree in Elementary Education. She taught first, second and third graders. After co-authoring creative drama books entitled CURTAIN I and CURTAIN II for Trillium Press, Sue presented a series of drama segments on the televised children's program "Hoorah for Kids!" Her creative time is divided between writing poems, activities, stories and books for educational publications.

Royal Fireworks Press
First Avenue
Unionville, NY 10988
(914) 726-4444
FAX: (914) 726-3824

Royal Fireworks Press
78 Biddeford Avenue
Downsview, Ontario
M3H 1K4
FAX: (416) 633-3010

ISBN: 0-88092-079-3

Printed in the United States of America by the Royal Fireworks Press of Unionville, New York.

TABLE OF CONTENTS

An Historic Moment

The man said,
after inventing poetry,
"WOW!"
and did a full somersault.

William J. Harris

A POEM IS JUST FOR YOU!

Read poetry. Remember poets' names. Copy favorite poems in a notebook or keep them in a card file. Read poems aloud to teachers, friends, parents and pets. *Cats love poetry.* Carry poems in your pockets. Pin poems in your room.

Learn the patterns and names for poetry devices. Learn poetry techniques so you can write a "prime time poem."

Poems begin with:

<u>ideas</u> ("I have an idea...let's")

<u>feelings</u> (my best friend *didn't* choose *me*)

<u>personal experiences</u> (I remember when I fell off the bus *right* in some mud and everyone...)

<u>objects</u> (a turquoise bracelet)

<u>nature</u> (watching a squirrel bite the shell off a hickory nut.)

There is no wrong or right way to write a poem. You can choose from many patterns or write free verse or create your own style.

Catch a Poem. Think of a subject or theme. Write down words that come into your head describing experiences, thoughts and feelings about that subject. You may write it only once or many times until the poem is just right for you.

Keep your poems. Read them from time to time. You will see how you have grown and changed as a person *and* as a poet.

ALPHABET VERSE

The first verse or poetry you read or listened to was alphabet verse. Alphabet verse starts with any letter of the alphabet (a through z) and describes one word beginning with that same letter. There may have been a picture of the word for you to color. This is alphabet verse:

<u>A</u> is an <u>a</u>pple

crunchy

red

apple

<u>K</u> stands for <u>k</u>ite

orange and white

nylon kite.

Hold on tight!

Write an alphabet verse.

- Choose any letter of the alphabet.
- Write as many words as you can think of beginning with that letter.
- Choose one of the words.
- Draw a picture of the word with crayon.

- Write the alphabet verse and describe what you see in the picture.

  <u>Use all of your five senses.</u> The sense of smell, taste, touch, hearing and what you see.

  <u>(b)</u> is a <u>   (balloon)   </u>

  _____

  _____

  _____

  _____

  _____

Write a Pizza Alphabet Verse.

- Close your eyes. Think about the smell of a pizza. What does it look like? What sound does it make when you bite into it? Pretend you are eating pizza. How does it taste and feel when you chew and swallow it? Did you use a napkin? Why?

- Draw a picture of the pizza you would order. What does it have on it? Put those ingredients in layers. Don't forget tomato sauce!

  P is for Pizza

  _____

  (how does it smell?)

  _____

  (what does it look like?)

  _____

  (what sounds do you hear while eating?)

  _____

  (how does it taste?)

  _____

  (how does it feel on your hand and in your mouth?)

  _____

  (name the kind of pizza you ordered)

Write a Best Friend Alphabet Poem.

Who is your best friend? Be with your best friend when you write this alphabet verse.

- Look at your best friend. Write words that describe him/her. What do you like to play together? What do you like *best* about your friend? What can he/she do that you wished *you* could do?

_____ stands for _____
    (letter)   (name)

_____

_____

_____

_____

_____

              _____
          (nickname)

Use your imagination when writing poetry. When you imagine something, you see a "picture" of it in your mind. Sometimes the picture is fanciful or not real. You can exaggerate to make the picture even *more* fanciful.

Write a zoo alphabet verse.

- Draw any *two* animals, birds or insects that you see at a zoo as *one* animal, bird or insect. An ocelot could have giant spider legs. An elephant could have peacock feathers. An ape could have a giraffe's neck. Write an alphabet poem about this imaginary creature.

- Name your zoo creature by dividing each selected animal, bird or insects name in half. Example: oce/lot, spi/der.

- Choose half of each name and write it together as one word. Example: spilot.

• Imagine where your creature lives, what it likes to eat, what sound it makes, what frightens it and if you would like it for a pet.

_____ is a _____
   (letter)   (animal)

M is for MASK

It changes a lot
To add a new face
To the face you have got;
Then the person you are
Is the person you're not.

m is for mask

William Jay Smith

A <u>poem</u> has rhythm and sometimes rhymes.

A <u>verse</u> is a section of one poem. A verse has rhythm and usually rhymes.

Alphabet Verse Books

There are a variety of ways to write alphabet verse. Discover other ways by reading these books.

ALFRED'S ALPHABET WALK
By Victoria Chess, Greenwillow Books, 1979

THE ABC OF BUMPTIOUS BEASTS
poems by Gail Kredenser, Harlin Quist, Inc.

TWO WORD POEM

A poem can be any length.

Some poems have hundreds of words and are many pages long. Some poems are as short as two words. These are two word rhyming poems:

I —
Why?

Eli Siegel

You.
Boo!

Anonymous

Karla Kuskin, a poet, was reading her poem "Bugs" from the book ALEXANDER SOAMES: HIS POEMS to a group of children. They said, "bugs. . .ugh." Is that a two word poem?

bugs
ugh(s)

Poems can rhyme or be non-rhyming.

These two word poems rhyme. They make a complete word picture. You can see the action or a complete description.

Examples:

hammer	sheep
clammer	leap

narrow	high
arrow	sky

sea	skunk
wheeeeeeee!	stunk

Write a Two Word Poem.

- Use a book or dictionary. Turn to any page. Find a word. Rhyme the word. Does it make a picture in your mind?

- Turn to another page. Find a word. Rhyme a word. Repeat.

- Write down the poems you like the best.

Write a Nonsense Two Word Poem.

<u>Nonsense words</u> are not found in the dictionary. They have no meaning. This poem has many nonsense words:

The True Names of the Months of the Year

Jammyway

Fibberway

Marts

Aprim

Moo

Joom

Jubly

Aw goo

Sembember

Oh coober

Mumnumber

Dreamember

Arnold Spilka

- Write nonsense words for the days of the week.

- Choose several for two word poems.

7

More Two Word Poems

- Use rhyming or non-rhyming words for Line 2.

Line 1 _____
            (long, long, long, long word)

Line 2 _____
            (a nonsense word)

****

Line 1 _____
            (name of your state)

Line 2 _____

****

Line 1 _____
            (a word for something you throw)

Line 2 _____

****

Line 1 _____
            (word for a vegetable you hate to eat)

Line 2 _____

There are two words in one line and several lines in this poem:

Bug in a Jug

Curious fly,

Vinegar jug,

Slippery edge,

Pickled bug.

Anonymous

- Write a *hat poem* with two words on one line. What kind of hat have you ever worn? Did you wear it because of the weather? Did you wear it for fun? Did you buy it in a store or at a Fair or amusement park? Describe the hat and where you wore it. Maybe it's magic!

Books with an Introduction to Poetry and Poems

KNOCK AT A STAR
by X.J. Kennedy and Dorothy M. Kennedy
Little, Brown & Co., 1982

DOGS AND DRAGONS, TREES AND DREAMS
by Karla Kuskin
Harper & Row, 1980

TONGUE TWISTERS

A tongue twister twists, tangles and tickles your tongue. The faster you go; the more the fun. A tongue twister repeats the same letter and combination of letters many times in one or more lines. What letter do you hear repeated in this tongue twister? Dennis didn't drink David's diet drink. The letter "d" was repeated. When a letter or blend of letters are repeated over and over in a sentence or line of poetry, it is called <u>alliteration</u> (al-lit-er-A-shun). Alliteration gives a beat or accent to verse and poetry. Say this tongue twister five times as fast as you can. "Chipmunk chomped on a chunk of cheddar cheese." Ask someone else to say it. Who said it the fastest?

An old tongue twister rhyme

Memorize "Betty Botter" and ask someone else to memorize it. Who says it the fastest...without making a mistake?

Betty Botter

Betty Botter bought some butter,

"But," said she, "this butter's bitter.

When I put it in my batter,

It makes all my batter bitter."

So she bought some better butter,

And put it in the bitter batter,

To make the bitter batter better.

Old Rhyme

Years ago, bards, poets and jesters used rhyming words and alliteration to help them memorize a poem or sing the lyrics in a song.

****

Create a tongue twister. Try remembering it without writing the words down. Memorize.

- Start with one word. Examples:

    turtle, Reggie, purple, ten, jogger.

- Choose another word beginning with the same sound. The second word tells something about the first word. Example:

    "Reggie's red"

- The second word can come before or after the first word. Now you have two words in your tongue twister!

- Choose another word beginning with the same sound. The repeated letter might be in the middle or last part of the word. Add it to the two words. Repeat the three words several times to help you remember.

- Continue adding words.

- Repeat the tongue twister aloud to others. Can they remember it? Have them repeat the tongue twister to you.

Write a tongue twister.

- Begin with one word. The beginning, middle or ending sound of that word will be repeated in other words. Use a blend (sh, ch, tr) or single letters.
  Example: "Floyd"

- Think of questions. Floyd what?
  Example: "Floyd flipped"

- Add another word asking a question. Floyd flipped what?
  Example: "Floyd flipped fish"

- Add another word by asking a question.
  Floyd flipped fish how?
  Example: "Floyd flipped fish fast"

- Continue asking questions, when, where, how, what, why. Words that do <u>not</u> have the repeated sound (alliteration) can also be used in a tongue twister.
  Example: "Floyd *could* flip fish faster *than* Fred." The words <u>could</u> and <u>than</u> did not repeat the "fl" or "f" sound.

Write tongue twisters about:

stretching string

cross cautiously

Gerry's gerbils

Fuzzy Freddy

Sherman's sheep

leaping lizards

double bubble

Try these tongue twisters:

Shave a cedar shingle thin.

* * *

Preshrunk shirts

* * *

Old, oily Ollie oils oily autos.

* * *

Sue's saw sawed Steve's seesaw.

* * *

Tom threw Tim three thumbtacks.

Tongue Twister Books

THE BIGGEST TONGUE TWISTER BOOK IN THE WORLD by Gales Brandeth, Sterling Publishing, 1980

PUCKS PECULIAR PET SHOP (A tongue twister story) by Dean Walley, Hallmark Children's Edition, publisher, 1970

FOX IN SOCKS by Dr. Seuss "A tongue twister for super children" Random House, Inc.

*The librarian will help you find other tongue twister books if these are not in your library.

JINGLES

Jingles are "bouncy" like bells jingling in a beat with rhythm. There are rhyming words in jingles. Do you jump rope? These are jump rope jingles:

"Teddy Bear, teddy bear, go upstairs"

****

"Hop on one foot; then on the other"

****

"Mabel, Mabel, set the table"

Write one more verse to a jump rope jingle.

- Choose a favorite jump rope jingle.

- Write the words down. Are there rhyming words? Where are they? How many lines in each verse?

- Write one more verse following the same pattern with rhyming words and number of lines in the verse.

****

Bounce a ball to this counting jingle:

One, two, three, O'Leary,

Four, five, six, O'Leary,

Seven, eight, nine, O'Leary,

Ten O'Leary,

Postman.

Old Jingle

Everyday you hear jingles advertising products on TV and radio. A jingle is spoken with rhythmic beat or sung to music. When a poem, jingle or verse is sung with music, it is called <u>lyrics</u>. Lyrics are words that accompany music.

****

Sing one of your favorite songs. Clap while you sing it. Does it have a steady beat? You are singing the *lyrics*...a poem.

****

Sing these jingles or say them while clapping:

"Krinkles Krunchies are crunchy and munchy.
Crunchy-munchy, crunchy-munchy,
crunchy-munchy, munchy-crunchy"

****

If you're hungry in your tummy

Try a candy bar with honey.

Your tummy gurgles back at you.

Yum, yum, yummy.

Write a jingle.

- What food do you like to eat? Is it a fruit, vegetable, meat, frozen food, canned or boxed? Does it have a brand name? Write the name of the food and the brand name. Write words describing all of the five senses when you eat it. Use your imagination. Write it with nonsense words. Be silly. Have fun writing your jingle!

- Sing or say the jingle while clapping.

- Send the jingle to the manufacturer of the product. The manufacturer's address is on the package.

Write a "y" jingle.

- Write the name of a person, object, fish, animal or insect.

- Write a word with action such as: crash, leap, scream, pound, punch, splash

- Add "y" to the end of all of the words.

Examples:

Silly Milly is _____

Terry is scary when _____

Witchey felly in the _____

Use words like: catchey, wetchey, fetchy, betchy, giggley spinkety-spankety, lopety-lankety, flippety, crumpety, lumpety, wiggley, floppy

Complete these jingles. Do them with a partner. Clap hands
together. Try to remember the verses without writing them.

Divey Oak-a, Divey Oak-a

Half past one

_____

_____

What happened at half past one?

Continue with half past two, then half past three. Continue with
half past each hour.

****

Chew-the-o

Hit the floor

Chew-the-o

_____

Chew-the-o

_____

****

Take a peach

Take a plum

Take a piece of bubble gum

_____ (create three or more lines)

Jingle Books

ONE WINTER NIGHT IN AUGUST AND OTHER
NONSENSE by X.J. Kennedy

Atheneum Press, 1975

FUNNY BONE TICKLERS IN VERSE AND RHYME

selected by Leland B. Jacobs

Garrard Publishing Company, 1973

LASAGNA

Wouldn't you love

To have lasagna

Any old time

The mood was on ya?

         X.J. Kennedy

FOUND POETRY

Printed words are found on boxes, labels, newspapers, catalogs, books, magazines and sacks. Words that are found, cut out and glued onto paper in a poem are <u>Found</u> Poetry. The words are any size, color, print or combination of those. The more shapes or letters and words you use will help to make the poem interesting and colorful.

*You need paper, scissors, glue and printed words for cutting out.

This poem was "found" in a catalog advertising a pinball game. The poet cut words out that were interesting and appealing.

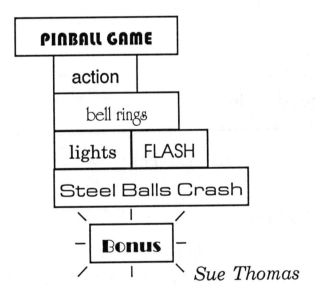

Sue Thomas

Find a Poem.

- Find printed words on one or several of the following: jar or can labels, boxes, newspaper, catalogs, magazines.

- Cut out single words or groups of words. What will the poem be about? Decide on a theme.

You may or may not title your poem. All poems do not have titles.

- Place the cut-out words in different arrangements.

- When your found poem is finished, glue it on the paper.

- Illustrate with crayons or felt pens.

Computer Giants

Running for cover
butting heads
carry them;
buckling
Squashed in
USA TODAY

Sue Thomas

Find A Number Poem.

- Find and cut out different sizes, shapes and colors of number signs: #, $, C, +, =; number words: four, thirty-one number names: 16, 125,000, 3

- Arrange the numbers on a sheet of paper. Cut out any additional words needed to complete the poem. Repeat words, names and signs.

- Possible themes or titles:

Fractured Fractions
No Cents
8%
The Money Machine
I'M RICH!
How Much is Many?
My Unlucky Number
Googol

- Glue down the final number poem arrangement.

- Illustrate your number poem.

A Clothes Found Poem

- Look in a newspaper or catalog for clothes you would buy if you were shopping. Cut the pictures out.

- Next, cut out words that describe the clothes you've chosen.

- Cut out the picture of a model that closely resembles you or draw a picture of yourself.

- Glue the model on the left hand side of a sheet of paper. Glue on the clothes and shoes you selected.

- Arrange the words on the right hand side of the paper that describe each article of clothing. The words should be placed approximately across from what is being described. Glue them down.

- The title for the poem could be your name or the "look" or style you have selected.

A Riddle Found Poem

- Find words that describe a holiday.
  Example: Halloween, Valentine's Day, Fourth of July, Mother's Day.

- Cut out all the words from the newspaper or magazine that describe how you feel about that day. What do you see on that day? What do you hear? Are there special activities that help you celebrate the day?

- Arrange the words into a pattern or lines. You may want to cut out more words to complete lines or complete thoughts.

- Glue the final arrangement on a sheet of paper. Keep the day you described a secret so when you exchange your poem with someone else, that person has to guess what holiday the riddle describes.

Narrative poems tell a story. One famous narrative poem is "Casey At the Bat" by Ernest Thayer. The story poem tells about a baseball player named Casey. All narrative poems, as in stories, have a beginning, a middle and an end.

A Movie Found Poem

- Look in a TV Guide, newspaper or magazine for advertisements of movies.

- Find a movie you want to attend.

- Cut out words from the ad that describe the movie. It will not tell the entire story. Use your imagination!

- Select and cut out more printed words telling the story the way you imagine it.

- Arrange the words in a <u>narrative poem</u>.

- Glue onto paper.

Attend the movie: Compare it to your imagined narrative poem.

A Four-Minute Found Poem

- Search for and cut out any words that appeal to you. Set a time limit of four minutes. Repeat the same word many times, if you like, or vary the sounds and length of each word.

- Lay the words down. Arrange them in different ways. Try to use every word in your poem.

- Can you find a theme or idea or story in the words? Is there a repeated rhythm or beat?

Look for a pattern. Examples:

> Repeat the same number of syllables on each line.

> Repeat the same number of words on each line.

> Repeat the same word, every other word or every fourth word.

> Repeat the same word again and again in the same line every third or fourth line.

- The last word or line tells the theme of the poem.
- Glue the poem onto paper.

****

WHO TO PET
AND WHO NOT TO

Go pet a kitten, pet a dog,

Go pet a worm for practice,

But don't go pet a porcupine—

You want to be a cactus?

> *X.J. Kennedy*

CHANTS

Poetry has rhythm. Rhythm is movement. There is rhythm in the way you breathe, gusts of wind blowing the trees, in music and dancing. A beat or accent comes and goes, then, comes and goes again. Sometimes the beat is heavy or loud; sometimes it is soft. Cheerleaders use chants at sports events. "E * A * S * T GO! GO! GO! GO!" A witch *always* mumbles a chant while mixing a secret potion or casting a spell. Chants repeat the same words over and over again in a rhythmic tone. Try nonsense words in a chant!

A Nonsense Chant

- Choose any letters and combine them into a nonsense word. Examples:

> cree-lo
>
> sup-sup-sup
>
> illy-illy
>
> rumbuggle
>
> polly-oooo

- Write words repeating the sounds or nonsense words into a four line chant.

  Example: creelo creelo
  > hey! hey! hey!
  >
  > creelo creelo
  > hey! hey! hey!

- Say the chant out loud *without* raising or lowering your voice. Then, *raise* and *lower* your voice using a steady beat or rhythm.

A Witch's Chant

- Start with:

  Bibbledy, bibbledy, babbledy, BOO!

  Here's what *I* put in witches brew!

- Continue the chant by telling what *you* would put in the brew.

- End the chant by repeating the first line: Bibbledy, bibbledy, babbledy, BOO!?

****

Winnie the Pooh likes "Outdoor Hums" as Pooh calls them in the book THE POOH STORY BOOK by A.A. Milne. D.P. Dutton & Co., 1956. Read "The More It Snows" found in Chapter I, page 8. Then, go outdoors. Skip or walk in a steady beat or rhythm. Does an "outdoor hum" come into your head like Pooh-bear's song?

PATCHWORD POETRY

Have you ever seen a patchwork quilt? It is a blanket made from pieces of different shapes, sizes and colors of material. A Patchwork or Patchword poem is also made from pieces of different shapes, sizes and colors. But instead of using material, the Patchwork poem uses words, letters and pictures.

*You need glue, scissors and paper to make a patchwork poem.

A Patchwork Poem

- Find a seed or toy catalog or an advertisement for a toy in the newspaper.

- Choose one advertisement. Cut out the picture and words that describe it. Cut out each word separately.

- Arrange the picture and words anywhere on the paper.

- Glue the final arrangement onto the paper.

Example:

LEMON FLUFF

Exotic flower
    large
        and
           glossy.
Golden beauty
    fluffy
       crinkly
         bouquet.

A Mosaic Patchword Poem

- Choose any picture from a comic book or a cartoon from the newspaper.

- Cut the picture into pieces like a puzzle.

- Glue the pieces of puzzle onto any color of paper. The pieces should look just like the picture or completed puzzle except for a narrow space between each piece...like mosaic tile. The colored paper shows through the narrow spaces. Let the mosaic dry.

- Find and cut out words that describe the cartoon or comic book picture.

- Arrange the words as a Patchword poem. Glue down.

****

A Leaf Patchword Poem

This is a "sound" poem. You will cut out single letters and blends of letters (2 or more letters together). The letters will be glued together to make words imitating sounds.

Find words that are in large print or type. Tiny or small letters are difficult to work with.

Poets sometimes combine letters to imitate or make a new word for a sound that is heard. This is called <u>onomatopoeia</u>. Pronounced (ON o MA toe pe E a). The words do not have any special meaning but they imitate the sound of something.

Examples: a machine sounds like "nyaaaaaaaaaaaaa"

       a rock hitting the water sounds like "guuuluump."

Your leaf patchwork poem will imitate sounds.

- Cut out single letters (not whole words), blends (str, ch, th), capital or small letters from headlines in newspapers or magazines. More letters may be needed.

- Combine the letters to make the sound of a leaf when:

Line 1 _____
        (a budding leaf opening in the spring)
Line 2 _____
        (the tiny new leaf growing bigger and bigger)
Line 3 _____
        (a caterpillar chewing on the leaf)
Line 4 _____
        (wind blowing the leaf back and forth against a branch)
Line 5 _____
        (rain beating steadily on the leaf)
Line 6 _____
        (an autumn leaf falling to the ground)
Line 7 _____
        (walking in autumn leaves)
Line 8 _____
        (raking leaves into a pile)
Line 9 _____
        (leaves burning in a bonfire)

* * * * * * * * * * * *

You made new words from sounds. Read the leaf poem aloud. It sounds like a secret code or the language from another planet. Only *you* know the secret of your onomatopoeia leaf poem.

COLLAGE POETRY

An artist's collage combines string, yarn, cloth, tissue paper, wood shavings or any variety of material. Pieces are layered on top of each other and in all different directions. Even upside down and sideways! Collage poetry uses scraps of a variety of materials and cut-out words.

- You will need liquid glue, thick paper, scissors, an old magazine, a black felt pen or crayon, and a paint brush.

- Prepare the glue by mixing it with water. ½ water and ½ glue.

A Color Collage Poem

- Choose any color.

- Cut pictures from magazines using different shades (light and dark) and objects in the chosen color.

- Find string, yarn, material or anything in your chosen color that can be glued onto thick paper.

- Arrange the pieces. Some can overlap. The pieces will be placed in different directions.

- Brush the glue mixture over each piece. Glue onto the paper.

- Tape the corners of the paper down until the collage dries.

- Cut out words that describe your color collage.

- The words will be scattered in different directions.

- Glue the words directly onto the collage for your Color collage poem.

Personification is a way of imagining objects. An object takes on life-like characteristics. An object becomes a person in your imagination. Have you ever heard a flower talk to you? Have you ever seen a frog dressed in clothes? Movies, television and stories use personification to make a story interesting. Poets use personification when writing poetry.

Dandelion

O little soldier with the golden helmet,

What are you guarding on my lawn?

You with your green gun

And your yellow beard,

Why do you stand so stiff?

There is only the grass to fight!

Hilda Conkling

The poet, Hilda Conkling, thinks about a dandelion as a soldier.

****

Look around the room. Pick out any five objects. Imagine each object doing something a person can do. The table might jiggle and shake and walk out of the room. A book grows arms and legs. A pencil is a dancing ballerina. Pieces of chalk are a marching band. Write personification ideas into a collage poem.

Is that the clock whispering?

PARODY

A <u>parody</u> mimics a song or poem that has already been written. Mimic means to copy someone or something. Comedians mimic people by poking fun at them and being silly. Charlie Brown and his friends in the cartoon strip "Peanuts" mimic and parody Christmas songs. They sing Halloween words in place of Christmas words. "Deck the halls with boughs of holly" is sung "Deck the patch with orange and black." "O Christmas Tree" is sung "Oh pumpkin cards."

Write a parody for the poem "Shopping"

Shopping

A bear and a bunny
Had plenty of money.
They went to the store
For carrots and honey.

When the bear and the bunny
Asked: "Carrots and honey?"
The man in the store
Cried: "Where is your money?"

How strange, and how funny!
They *really* had money—
And that's how they bought
Their carrots and honey!

                    Ilo Orleans

Decide who your parody will be about. It could be two other animals, two toys, two people or two super heroes.

A _____ and a _____

Had plenty of _____.

They went to the _____

For _____ and _____.

When the _____ and the _____

Asked: "_____?"

The _____ in the _____

Cried: "_____?"

How strange and how funny!

They _____

And that's how they _____

Their _____ and _____!

Write a Mother Goose Parody.

• Read Mother Goose poems. Select one or more to parody.

Mother Goose Poetry Books

THE MOTHER GOOSE TREASURY, selected by Raymond Biggs; Coward, Mc Cann, 1966

MOTHER GOOSE pictures by Tasha Tudor, Walck, 1944

- Write any Mother Goose poem leaving blanks for the words you will write "updating" the rhyme.

  Examples:

  > Jack and Jill went (up in a rocket).
  >
  > Humpty Dumpty sat on a (diving board).
  >
  > Little Bo-Peep has lost her (lunch money).
  >
  > Pussy cat, pussy cat, where have you been?
  >
  > I've been to a (movie).
  >
  > There was an old woman who lived in (Disneyland).
  >
  > Simple Simon met (a TV star).

Write a song Parody.

- Choose a song.

- Write the words or lyrics leaving spaces for your "updated" version.

- Fill the blanks with your own choice of words.

Parody Poetry Books

> THE CHARLES ADDAMS MOTHER GOOSE
>
> Harper & Row, 1967
>
> THE SPACE CHILD'S MOTHER GOOSE,
>
> by Frederick Winsor, Simon and Schuster, 1956.
>
> THE CITY AND COUNTRY MOTHER GOOSE,
>
> by Hilde Hoffman, American Heritage Press, 1969.

CONCRETE POETRY

Concrete poems are seen and read at the same time. The words in the poem make a picture (shape) of the subject or theme. The words are sometimes written to show action.

WHEE

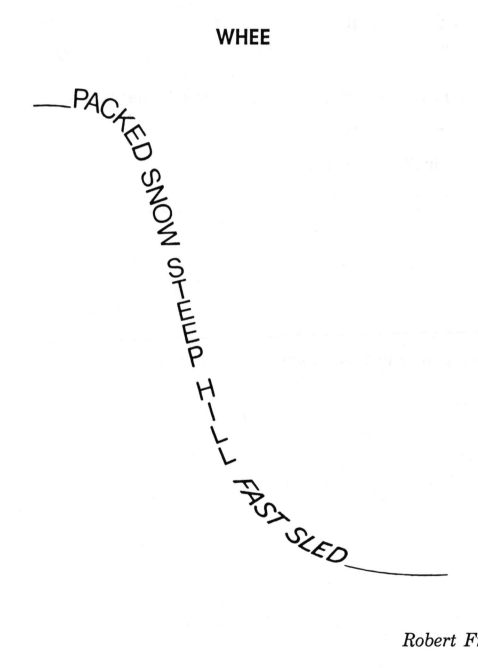

Robert Froman

Write shaped words

Examples: small   BIG

t   t
w   w
i   i
n   n
s   s

snake

- Write these words in their shape or words that you choose.

hot	windy
giraffe	caterpillar
thin	pencil
curly	sandwich
long	snow

- Write actions in their shape.

Examples:

$$J \; U \; M \; P \; I \; N \; G$$

$$h^o p \quad h^o p \quad h^o p \quad h^o p$$

Write these action poems or any action ideas you choose.

Use the words <u>jump rope</u> and <u>hop</u> up and down to show someone jumping rope.

Use the word <u>basketball</u> and <u>dribble</u> showing a basketball being dribbled.

Use the word <u>hammer</u> and <u>nail</u> showing a nail being driven into something with a hammer.

Shape a Candy Bar Concrete Poem.

- Buy your favorite Candy Bar. Cut it in half.

- Lightly sketch an outline of the shape of your candy bar in pencil. Show the layers of ingredients. You might want to include the wrapper on the outside edge of your drawing.

- Write words along the pencil lines that describe the ingredients. Think how it tastes and feels. Write those words on the candy bar. What do you hear when you bite into the bar? Write those words on the candy bar pencil sketch.

- Lightly color the different ingredients with crayons or colored pencils.

Write an Action Concrete Poem.

Example:

chocolate
ice
cream
cone

choc lick
ice lick
cream
cone

lick lick
lick ice lick
cream
cone

lick
lick lick
cream
cone

lick
lick lick
cone

lick
crunch
cone

crunch
cone

crunch

Sue Thomas

Choose one of these ideas or try *your* own creative idea!

subject	action
balloon	air coming out...deflating
kite	jerked by strong wind
shark	chasing you
leaf	crunching under your foot

A Newspaper Concrete Shaped Poem

You will need scissors, black felt pen, glue, newspaper and a large sheet of plain paper.

- Find one interesting article in the newspaper. What is the main subject or theme of the article?

- Cut the article in the shape of that theme. Draw a pencil outline of the shape as large as is possible and then cut out. A football game article would be cut into the shape of a football. A zoo article would be cut into the shape of the animal it was written about. A story about a building would be cut into the shape of a building.

- Glue the shape onto plain paper.

- Find words in the article that tell about and show ACTION.

- Write those words in black felt pen on the newspaper shape for your concrete poem.

A German poet wrote this concrete poem. Can you find a surprise in the Apfel or apple poem?

ApfelApfelApfelApfel
ApfelApfelApfelApfelA
ApfelApfelApfelApfelApfe
ApfelApfelApfelApfelApfelApf
ApfelApfelApfelApfelApfel
ApfelApfelApfelApfelApfe
ApfelApfelApfelApfelApfelA
ApfelApfelApfelApfelApfe
ApfelApfelApfelApfelApfel
ApfelApfelApfelApfelApf
ApfelApfelApfelWurmAp
ApfelApfelApfelApfel
ApfelApfelApfel
ApfelApfelA
Apfel

Reinhard Döhl

Concrete Poetry Books

SEEING THINGS a book of poems written and designed by Robert Froman, Thomas Y. Crowell

POP POEMS by Ronald Gross, Simon & Schuster, 1967

SIMILE

A simile compares two unlike things using *like* or *as* when comparing them.

Examples:

The spaghetti looked <u>like</u> worms.

The cookie was <u>as</u> chewy <u>as</u> a caramel.

****

These are simile comparisons written by boys and girls. They were published in the magazine <u>Ranger Rick</u>, December, 1977.

Snow is like a little frisky
filly when it dances in the
wind.

Alison Church
Homer, NY

Snow is a whirlwind of
white dots.

Darriel Frost
Homer, NY

Snow is angels' tears freezing
as they fall.

Chris Stoughton
Homer, NY

Compare two unlike things:

Her truck was silver like a _____ .

The _____ was salty like _____ .

The string was knotted like a _____ .

Pete is twisting like a _____ .

The _____ was junky like _____ .

_____ was growing like _____ .

_____ was puckered like _____ .

The vase was ugly like _____ .

The _____ was grassy like a _____ .

My cat was as cuddly as _____ .

The horn was as noisy as _____ .

My room was as icy as _____ .

His horse was as wild as _____ .

The yard was as rocky as _____ .

The levi's were as tight as _____ .

Ron's hair was as curly as _____ .

Her TV Dinner was as frozen as _____ .

This simile poem was written by a third grade boy.

Dark as night

Dark as a room without light

Dark as when you lose your sight

Is a cloudy day.

Brad Sloan
Columbia, Mo.

Write a Simile Poem.

There can be as many lines as you choose to write. The verse can rhyme or be non-rhyming. Examples:

As _____ as _____

As _____ as _____

As _____ as _____

Is (or Are) _____

****

My braces are like _____

_____

_____

When _____

****

I feel like _____

I feel like _____

I feel like _____

When _____

Simile Poem Themes:

chili	roller skates	pockets
baby whale	fence	goldfish
hairy ape	new shoes	haircut
barefoot	a birthday present	jelly beans

METAPHOR

Pronounced (MET a for). A metaphor compares two different things but the word <u>like</u> or <u>as</u> is *not* necessary as in a simile poem.

****

Sometimes in telling a story a person will exaggerate to make a point or to make the story more interesting. In poetry, there is a word for exaggeration to make a point. The word is <u>hyperbole</u> (hi PUR bul lee). Hyperbole is written into simile or metaphor poems to make a comparison between two things.

Example: "His heart is as big as his body."

The writer helps you understand how very kind-hearted the person is. Hyperbole or exaggeration helps to make a point.

What does the poet compare with "dragon smoke" on a cold day in the following poem?

DRAGON SMOKE

Breathe and blow
white clouds
      with every puff.

It's cold today,
      cold enough
to see your breath.

Huff!
      Breathe dragon smoke
        today!

Lilian Moore

Write a Metaphor Poem.

- Choose one thing you are interested in. Do you have a hobby? Do you have a pet? What is your favorite sport? Who is your favorite cartoon character?

- Think what you would compare with your choice. Exaggerate!

   Ideas for your poem:

    Compare snow to popcorn

    a turtle shell to your house

    a fireman's hose to a snake

    an insect to a space invader

    an ice cream sundae to a mountain

    a car to a beetle

    a road to a ribbon

    ocean waves to a person's tongue

    clouds to _____

This poet compares rain to a mouse.

Rain Poem

The rain was like a little mouse,

quiet, small and gray.

It pattered all around the house

and then it went away.

It did not come, I understand,

indoors at all, until

it found an open window and

left tracks across the sill.

Elizabeth Coatsworth

Poetry Books including Metaphor Poems

IT DOESN'T ALWAYS HAVE TO RHYME by Eve
Merriam, Atheneum, 1964

GREEN IS LIKE A MEADOW OF GRASS selected by
Nancy Larrick, Garrard Publishing

KENNING

Years ago, the English and Norsemen wrote metaphor in verses. The verses are Kenning poems. Begin the poem with a hyphenated compound word (grey-like) or two words using a hyphen to describe one word in another way.

Example:

a cherry	lipstick-ball
the sky	lost-lake
candy	sweet-rock
ice	slick-wax

Write a verse describing a Kenning Poem.

"Lost-Lake"

Look up

In the sky

A lost-lake!

"Sweetrock"

Cinnamon, HMMMMM!

Crunch, suck,

Sweet-rock's gone.

Write a metaphor comparison using a hyphenated compound word for the following:

moon

Saturday

school

ladybug

koala bear

toaster

strawberry

crocodile

ribbon

rose (flower)

* * * * * * * * * * * * *

Write a Kenning Verse.

Choose one or several of the words above. The Kenning can rhyme or be non-rhyming. *You* are the poet. *You* decide what to write about and how to write your poem. Poets rewrite their poems many times. Words are added or dropped. The "first" idea for the poem may be changed or take on new meaning. You may write your poem over and over until it says exactly what you want it to say.

Stories in Verse Books

A DAY IN THE COUNTRY by Willis Barnstone
Harper & Row, 1971

A GIRAFFE AND A HALF by Shel Silverstein
Harper & Row, 1964

ACROSTIC

Acrostic poetry was written in ancient times. The subject or theme of an acrostic poem is written vertically one letter at a time in a column. Each letter begins a word, a phrase or a sentence on that line of poem. Examples:

s	f	r	m	s
n	r	o	o	o
a	e	l	s	c
i	e	l	q	c
l	b	e	u	e
	i	r	i	r
	e	s	t	
	s	k	o	
		a		
		t		
		e		
		s		

The first letter in each line is the first letter in the word that begins the line.

Experiences you have had in the past will give you ideas in writing poems. It would be difficult to write about a snail if you have never seen one. It would be difficult to write about roller skating if you have never roller skated. Choose subjects for your poems that you know something about or have had some experience with.

This is an acrostic verse:

Extinct?
Almost. *Our*
Glorious
Legendary
Everlasting
Symbols.

Sue Thomas

Write an Acrostic Poem.

- Choose something you know about or have had some experience with. You may change the words many times before you are satisfied with the poem.

- Write the letters of the word you've chosen in a vertical line. Each begins a new line.

Write a Name Acrostic Verse.

- Write your name in single letters vertically on paper. Choose your nickname or full name. Leave a space between your first and last name just as you would when writing it down.

- Describe what you look like, what you like to do, about your brothers and sisters or any special talents you have.

Try writing a Crossword Acrostic.

Short words are used two times to form a square as in a crossword puzzle. The repeated word is written both across and down the square.

Example: *sun
          use
          net

49

- Decide on one short word to begin the acrostic.

- Write the word across (horizontally) and down (vertically) using the first letter in the left hand corner. (see the *)

- Write the second word both across and down (the word <u>use</u> in the example).

- Add one last letter (see circled letter) to complete the verse.

Write a Game Acrostic Poem.

Examples:

```
m        d        c        s        l        c
o        u        h        c        i        h
n        n        e        r        f        e
o        g        c        a        e        s
p        e        k        b                 s
o        o        e        b
l        n        r        l
y        s        s        e

         a
         n
         d

         d
         r
         a
         g
         o
         n
         s
```

50

COUPLET

A couplet is a verse with <u>two</u> lines. One poem can have many couplets.

Each line ends in a rhyming word. Examples:

Who dat?
Standin' on ma mat?

I quit
you're it.

Rhyme a word with the following words:

skunk	burro	soul	nut	fly
syrup	jelly	orbit	face	gold
lamb	pond	sing	comb	ape
I	sorry	hurt	sail	hair
chord	me	other	found	cave
octopus	seashell			

Write a Couplet.

- Choose two words that rhyme from the list above or use two other words.

- Write the first line using one rhyming word.

- Write the second line using the other rhyming word.

Start with several of these following lines:

I saw a monster fly

_____

There grew a golden tree

_____

I looked in the _____

_____

When the telephone rang,

_____

What! A valentine for me?

_____

St. Patrick's Day comes once a year

_____

Sizzle and fry

_____

BLUE WOOL MONKEY

The blue wool monkey won't sit where
We put him in the rocking chair.

He likes it better on my bed
Where he can tumble on his head

And somersault upon the floor
To see who's coming in the door.

Myra Cohn Livingston

TERCET VERSE

Pronounced (TUR set). Tercet verse has three lines. The rhyming patterns are:

Pattern #1   All three lines rhyme.

    Example: I was drinking a *coke*.
                  My friend told a *joke*.
                  It made me *choke*.

Pattern #2   The first and second line rhyme.

    Example: Tom liked *Chris*.
                  He gave her a *kiss*.
                  She didn't like it!

Pattern #3   No lines rhyme

    Example: I *really* do like school!
                  At least, I *think* I do.
                  Maybe, just *some* days.

Think about these ideas for writing a tercet verse:

excuses   Why you forgot your gym shoes.
                  Why you dropped the glass.
                  Why you ran into something.
                  Why you lost the book.

<u>pies</u>	Would you eat one? What kind?
	Would you throw one? Who at?
	Would you step in one? Why?
<u>monster</u>	Is it friendly, mean, cross,
	selfish, unhappy, sloppy,
	careless, shy, stupid, fat
	silly, weird
<u>clothes</u>	What color do you like best?
	Do you like old clothes or new clothes?
	Do you wear the "latest fad"?
	Can you buy all the clothes you want?
<u>angry</u>	What makes you angry? Why?
	How do you show your anger?
	Do you get angry with yourself? Why?
<u>lucky day</u>	What happened today that was lucky for you?
	Are you always lucky?
	Are you superstitious about luck?
	Are you <u>ever</u> lucky?
<u>potatoes</u>	(chips, fries, mashed, baked, escalloped, fried)
	Have you ever cooked a potato?
	How did you cook it? Was it good?
	Did you use a recipe? Who ate it?
	Where do you order potatoes?

Write a Tercet Verse.

- Decide on one of the three patterns.

- Choose one of the ideas or something you choose to write about. There can be *more* than one tercet verse in a poem. Write more verses!

Stanza is a group of lines forming a section of a poem or song. A stanza is similar to a paragraph in a story. A stanza in a poem divides "thoughts."

This tercet verse has four stanzas.

Tag Along

Sing song
Tag along
Standing by the wall

Crank pot
Whine a lot
Just because you're small

Big shot
Red hot
Go and wilt a flower

Rough tough
Mean enough
To make the milk turn sour

Nina Payne

David McCord is a well-known poet. He has written many poetry books and received awards for his excellence in writing children's poetry. He writes humorous verse and poems about nature. Mr. McCord suggests that you read your poem aloud many times as you write it. In his book ONE AT A TIME, he explains how to write poetry. "Gone" is one of his tercet poems written about a lost dog. "The Tercet" another poem, tells about writing in the tercet pattern.

Read poems from:

ONE AT A TIME; His collected poems for the young
by David McCord, Little, Brown & Co., 1974

QUATRAIN

Pronounced (KWA train). A quatrain is a four-lined verse. You can write a quatrain with no rhyming words or write a quatrain in a pattern using rhyming words.

Remember   A <u>couplet</u> is <u>two</u> lines
                      A <u>tercet</u> is <u>three</u> lines
                      A <u>quatrain</u> is <u>four</u> lines

These are <u>rhyming</u> patterns for a quatrain:

Pattern #1   Line 1 (a) and line 4 (a) rhyme.
   Example: Line 1 _____ (a)
              Line 2 _____ (b)
              Line 3 _____ (c)
              Line 4 _____ (a)

Pattern #2   Line 1 (a) and line 2 (a) rhyme.
              Line 3 (b) and line 4 (b) rhyme.
   Example: Line 1 _____ (a)
              Line 2 _____ (a)
              Line 3 _____ (b)
              Line 4 _____ (b)

Pattern #3   Line 2 (b) and line 4 (b) rhyme.
   Example: Line 1 _____ (a)
              Line 2 _____ (b)
              Line 3 _____ (c)
              Line 4 _____ (b)

Pattern #4 Line 1 (a) and line 3 (a) rhyme.
     Line 2 (b) and line 4 (b) rhyme.

Example: Line 1 _____ (a)
     Line 2 _____ (b)
     Line 3 _____ (a)
     Line 4 _____ (b)

Pattern #5 Line 1 (a) and line 4 (a) rhyme.
     Line 2 (b) and line 3 (b) rhyme.

Example: Line 1 _____ (a)
     Line 2 _____ (b)
     Line 3 _____ (b)
     Line 4 _____ (a)

I've Got a Dog

I've got a dog as thin as a rail,

He's got fleas all over his tail;

Every time his tail goes flop,

The fleas on the bottom all hop to the top.

Anonymous

Write a Quatrain Verse.

There's a _____

Sitting on a _____

Sipping on _____

_____

****

The dog _____

The cat _____

and the mouse _____

_____

Choose any of the following lines for the <u>first line</u> in a quatrain. Your quatrain verse can be non-rhyming or follow a rhyming pattern. There may be one of more stanzas.

> I went to visit grandma'

> _____ fell in the pool

> A swaying bridge was _____

> I can do anything with a wire

> If you step on a crack

> I rode my bike on the ice

> The swing CRACKED

> Hiking is <u>only</u> fun

> Hey! That ball is mine

> My scooter has stripes

> I'm gonna' dump this stuff

> These peanuts are stale

> Where'd you get those eyes?

THE RANDOM HOUSE BOOK OF POETRY Selected by
Jack Prelutsky, Random House, 1983

This poet wrote a poem with a couplet, a tercet <u>and</u> a quatrain
stanza in one poem. You can, too!

Hey, Bug!

Hey, Bug, stay!
Don't run away.
I know a game that we can play.

I'll hold my fingers very still
and you can climb a finger-hill.

No, no.
Don't go.

Here's a wall—a tower, too,
a tiny bug town, just for you.
I've a cookie. You have some.
Take this oatmeal cookie crumb.

Hey, bug, stay!
Hey, bug!
Hey!

Lilian Moore

CLERIHEW

A clerihew is quatrain verse (four lines). The lines will vary in length. The pattern is: rhyme lines 1 and 2 (a) and lines 3 and 4 (b). The clerihew is written about a person. The first line of the poem is the person's name.

Pattern: Line 1 and 2 (a) rhyme.
              Line 3 and 4 (b) rhyme.

Example: Line 1 _____ (a)
                     (person's full name)
              Line 2 _____ (a)

              Line 3 _____ (b)

              Line 4 _____ (b)

****

A ROYAL EVENT

George Brett

mad? You *bet.*

When the umpire ruled in a gravel-voiced shout,

"Pine tar's too high on that bat. YOU'RE OUT!"

Sue Thomas

Write a Clerihew.

- Choose one person. Write her/his proper name on the first line.

- Tell something biographical about the person. Something that has happened in the person's life. Line 2 rhymes with line one. Line 2 can be any length.

- Line three and line four tell more about the biographical incident or happening. Line three rhymes with line 4.

A Folk Hero Clerihew:
    Paul Bunyon

    John Henry

    Pecos Bill

    Other

A Frontiersmen Clerihew:
    Daniel Boone

    Davey Crockett

    Jim Bowie

    Other

A Sports Figure Clerihew:
    Mario Andretti

    Reggie Jackson

    Mary Lou Retton

    John McEnroe

    Other

A President of the United States Clerihew

Abraham Lincoln

Richard Nixon

Bill Clinton

Dwight Eisenhower

A <u>You</u> Clerihew

There is no way to predict the future, BUT, what might *you* be famous or world renowned for? You could discover a new planet, be a world-renowned dancer, a TV star, cure a fatal disease or be in <u>Guinness Book of World Records</u> for building the biggest snow castle.

FREE VERSE

Free verse is a thought or idea written down in no particular style or pattern. The poet lets ideas flow freely and writes them down in single words or groups of words. There may be no punctuation marks such as periods, commas and question marks. This free verse was written by a young girl.

KATIE'S SHADOW POEM

don't step on my shadow

it's a magic coat I carry with me

you will fall into it,
you will fall down
      a hundred stairs
and a man with desert in his hair
will come and get you

you will be sorry,
for he is my grandfather's grandfather

he will tell you:
this is what happens
when you step on my shadow

Katie Vinz
Moorhead, Minnesota

Write a Free Verse Shadow Poem.

Consider what would happen if someone stepped on *your* shadow. Maybe something magical or silly or bad. Perhaps, you could tell about a game of Shadow Tag in your poem. Do you make hand shadows on the wall? Tell about your shadow "puppet" or figure.

Write a Greeting Card Free Verse.

You buy greeting cards for special occasions. When did you buy one the last time? Was it your father's birthday or Valentine's Day? Think what the occasion was and who you bought the card for. Write your own free verse for that "special occasion."

Ideas for other free verse poems. Pretend it's happening to you:

- Soap is in all the faucets. When the water is turned on, soap bubbles come out.

- A pumpkin tells its story about being planted as a seed, growing as a plant being sold and carved into a jack-o-lantern. *Then,* what happens to it?

- You live inside a squirrel's nest with two brothers and a sister. Your tails get tangled together.

- You have been invited for lunch with the President of the United States in Washington,D.C. THE WHITE HOUSE. What will you talk about? What will you wear? What will they serve for lunch?

- You are standing in the middle of a bridge. The steel supports begin to lean out. You are sinking fast. There is a gorge below...with no water.

- You dive off a high board into a pool filled with cherry jello looking for the key to a treasure chest. How does the jello feel in your ears and eyes? Will you lick it off or take a shower? Did you find the key?

LIMERICK

A Limerick is like a jingle. It is silly and fun to write. There are five rhythmic lines. The first, second and fifth line rhyme. The third and fourth line rhyme. There is also a pattern for the number of syllables in each line. You may or may not follow the pattern for syllables.

Pattern   Line 1 (a), 2 (a) and 5 (a) rhyme.
                    Line 3 (b) and 4 (b) rhyme.

Example: Line 1 _____ (a)
                  (8 or 9 syllables)
           Line 2 _____ (a)
                  (8 or 9 syllables)
           Line 3 _____ (b)
                  (5 or 6 syllables)
           Line 4 _____ (b)
                  (5 or 6 syllables)
           Line 5 _____ (a)
                  (8 or 9 syllables)

There was a young farmer of Leeds,

Who swallowed six packets of seeds.

It soon came to pass

He was covered with grass,

And he couldn't sit down for the weeds.

Unknown

There was an old man of Peru,

66

Who dreamt he was eating his shoe.

He awoke in the night

In a horrible fright,

And found it was perfectly true!

Unknown

* * * * * * * * * * *

Rhyme line 1, 2 and 5.

I once met a bear in the _____

He carried a jar full of _____

I asked him, "What for?"

He replied with a roar,

" _____."

Rhyme line 3 and 4.

A lazy young boy named Ned.

Didn't want to get out of bed.

His mother said, "_____

_____

Ned *got* out of bed. *Just* like she said.

67

Write a Limerick.

- Begin with one of the following first lines or create your own:

> The planet of apes was jumpin'
> A hamburger said to the bun
> I have a young cousin named _____
> Fifty ants marched down the road
> When I sat on the bench it said, "Ouch!"
> A video game called _____
> The first man who walked on the moon
> A dog with green legs and red ears
> Oh! Oh! _____. I'm late to school
> There once was a magical mirror
> I swallowed the wiggling worm
> A coach by the name of _____
> It lived in a cage at the zoo

- Think of a rhyme for the last word in the first line. Write a second sentence ending with the rhyming word.

- Rhyme words for line 3 and 4. Write sentences ending with those words.

- Rhyme line 5 with line 1 and 2.

Limerick Books

LAUGHABLE LIMERICKS compiled by Sara and John E. Brewton, T.Y. Crowell, 1965

THERE ONCE WAS A BOOK OF LIMERICKS by Paul Sawyer, Raintree Children's Books, 1978

TRIANGULAR TRIPLET

Have you talked about or made a triangle in mathematics? A Triangular Triplet is a triangle shaped poem. Triplet means three. This poem has a shape as in concrete poetry but the shape does not have the meaning or theme of the poem. This is a Triangular Triplet poem:

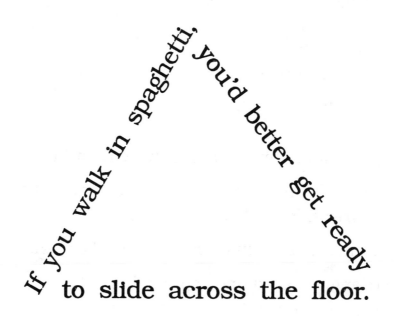

If you walk in spaghetti, you'd better get ready to slide across the floor.

There are three lines. Each line is one side of the triangle. You might want to start the first line on another side of the triangle. You are the poet. It will be easier for the person that reads it, if you write the lines consecutively or one after the other.

Write a Triangular Triplet Poem.

- The poem will have three lines almost equal in length. Choose from one of these ideas or write from your own experience. Think about walking barefoot in:

> hot desert sand
> sticky molasses
> slippery ice
> squishy mud
> straw
> slimy moss
> rocky lake bottom
> peanut butter
> cold snow

- When the poem is written, measure the longest line.

- Lightly draw a triangle using the measurement of the longest line. Each of the three sides will be that length.

- Write the poem along the lines in dark pencil or pen.

- Erase the triangle shaped line. (optional)

Write a many-lined Triangle Shaped Poem.

The words form the shape of a triangle.

> giggles
> bubble up inside me
> spilling over; spilling out
> bursting, spurting silly sounds

> *Sue Thomas*

Start with one word. Each line will be longer than the last line. That makes the shape of the triangle. There can be three sentences or more. Write until your poem is complete. Your triangle can fill an entire page and have many lines.

Experiment with different shapes of poems. The poems could be shaped like a star, square, hexagon, rectangle or circle. Try drawing the shape first.

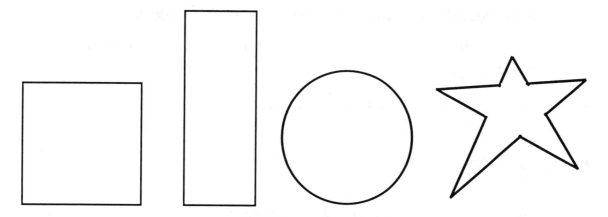

Write a Dream Triangular Triplet Poem.

- Have you had a dream that was frightening? It must be a dream *you* have had. Was it dark? Did something happen to someone you love? Were you falling? Was something falling on you? Use imagination and make it even *more* scary. Tell about it.

- Make several triangles one inside the other.

- Begin writing on the outside triangle and finish writing on the inside triangle.

- The triangles can be any size. Example:
- Start writing at any corner.
- Erase the penciled triangle lines (optional).

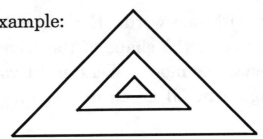

What if:

> you opened a door and dropped into anotherworld?

> you were locked inside a candy shop all night?

> you traded places with your mother, father,sister or brother for one hour?

> you grew the wings of a bat and could fly?

Poetry Books

BRONZEVILLE BOYS AND GIRLS,
by Gwendolyn Brooks, Harper & Row, 1956

SEE MY LOVELY POISON IVY by Lilian Moore
Atheneum Press, 1975

DIAMANTE or diamite

Pronounced (dee ah MAHN tay). Diamante is a french word meaning diamond. This poem is shaped like a diamond. There are seven lines. The words shape the pattern.

		Number of words
Line 1	(noun)	1
Line 2	(adjective,adjective)	2
Line 3	(verb, verb, verb)	3
Line 4	(noun, noun, noun, noun)	4
Line 5	(verb, verb, verb)	3
Line 6	(adjective,adjective)	2
Line 7	(noun)	1

A diamite or diamante poem uses parts of speech.

noun ...a person, place, thing or condition

adjective ...a word that tells about or describes a person, place or thing.

verb ...an action word that shows doing, being or happening.

*See the slash mark in the middle of Line 4. The slash mark divides the poem's contrasting subjects. The first half (before the slash mark) is written about one subject. The second half (after the slash mark) is written about an opposite subject.

The first half of this poem was written about <u>rain</u>. The second half or opposite subject is <u>sun</u>.

rain

wet, drops

splishing, dripping, splashing

thunder,   storm / rays,   beams

shining, streaking, shimmering

golden, hot

Sun

Subjects could be:

First half	Second half
night	day
summer	winter
sunny day	rainy day
happy	sad
mother	father
friend	enemy
earth	space
country	city

Write a Diamante Poem.

- Decide on two opposite subjects.

- Write as many words as you can think of that describe each one.

- Which of these are adjectives, verbs and nouns? On which line would each be placed to fit the pattern? *You do not have to follow the parts of speech on a special line. You *can* just write words that describe the noun (or subject) on any line in the half describing that subject.

Step by Step

1. Lightly number seven lines with pencil.
2. Write one word the noun (or subject) on Line 1 and Line 7. They are the middle points of the diamond shape. The two nouns have opposite meanings.
3. Write two adjectives on Line 2 and 6 that describe each subject.
4. Write three verbs on Line 3 and 5 that describe each subject.
5. Write four nouns on line 4. The first two describe the first half of the poem. The last two describe the last half of the poem. you may or may not make a slash mark.
6. Erase the numbers.
7. *Remember.* The poem is diamond shaped.

Write an Animal Diamante Poem.

- Choose one animal to write about. The first part of the poem is the animal as a baby. The last part of the poem is the animal as an adult. All things change as they grow. Subjects (nouns) could be:

Young Animal	Adult
duckling	duck
fawn or doe	deer
chick	chicken or rooster
kitten	cat
puppy	dog
piglet	hog or pig
lamb	sheep
colt	horse

- Write the young animal's name on Line 1.

- Write the adult animal's name on Line 7.

- The first half of the poem *before* the slash mark (/) will describe the young animal. The last half of the poem *after* the slash mark will describe the adult animal.

- Complete the other lines using the parts of speech or putting any descriptive words on any line.

Other subjects for Diamante poems are:

You   Write <u>baby</u> on the first line and your <u>first name</u> on the last line. What changes have you gone through as you have grown? You have more teeth, longer arms and your feet keep growing.

Mother   Write "<u>mom</u>" on the first line or mommy, whatever you call your mother. The last line (line 7) can be her <u>first name</u> or the word <u>mother</u>.

Pet   Your <u>pet</u> might be a cat, hog, squirrel, horse, pigeon, python. Write the word for the bird, animal or reptile on the first line. Write the <u>name</u> you call the pet by on the last line (line 7).

HAIKU

Pronounced (hi koo). Haiku is an oriental form of writing poetry in Japan. These poems usually describe seasons of the year. Haiku has three non-rhyming lines. There is a pattern for the number of English language syllables if you choose to write your Haiku poem following the pattern.

Pattern: Line 1 _____
                        (5 syllables)
            Line 2 _____
                        (7 syllables)
            Line 3 _____
                        (5 syllables)

*You can write the three lines of verse following the syllable pattern on each line. Or, any number of syllables can be on each line with the <u>total</u> numbering <u>17</u> <u>syllables</u>.

Summer Wind

Breath of a dragon,

Whispering round my window—

The soft summer wind.

Barbara Johnson
Age 13

Flowers are fragile

And like the soft, soft velvet

of a horse's nose.

Debra Jeffers

Grade 7

The toad! It looks as if

It would belch forth

A cloud!

— *Issa*

****

Haiku poetry brings vivid images into the mind of the reader. Imagery is important when writing poetry. The words in a poem describe a picture or image. Re-read the Haiku poems. The word "whispering" in "Summer Wind" describes how quietly the wind is blowing. The word "velvet" in the poem about flowers describes how soft the flower feels. "Belch forth" helps the reader imagine how fat and full the toad is. Use words in poetry that help the reader use all their five senses. Use words in Haiku that help the reader picture what is being written about. Choose several seasonal changes listed below and portray vivid images of the seasons.

Seasonal Changes

Autumn Images

Harvest moon . . big orange ball
cocoons . . caterpillars spinning
grasshoppers and ants . . store food
harvest time . . crops ripen and are harvested
frost . . flowers and plants die
leaves . . change color
birds . . fly south to warmer climates
pumpkins and apples . . sold at roadside stands
animals, reptiles . . hibernate

Winter Images

lakes, ponds and streams . . freeze . . .
time for ice skating and ice hockey
Jack Frost . . paints pictures
snow . . skiing, snowmen, sledding
animals . . grow heavy fur coats
trees and bushes . . bare branches
stars . . the big dipper, orion, the twins
blizzards . . snow whips into drifts
fireplace . . logs burning

Spring Images

leaves . . bud out
grass . . turns green
birds . . fly north . . baby birds in nests
fish . . tadpoles in creeks
animals . . awaken from hibernation
rain . . storms, showers, drizzle, sleet
fruit trees . . blossom
hurricanes . . slam against coast lines
kites . . fly in chilling winds

flowers . . crocus and daffodils bloom
fields . . farmers plow and plant seed

Summer Images

flies . . buzzing
fireflies . . flickering lights
birds . . feed on worms
bees . . sip honey from flowers
slugs and snails . . on damp wet ground
squirrels . . leaping from branch to branch
water . . swimming pool
apples and peaches . . ripen orchards
ocean . . waves beating the shore
snakes . . slither through grass

Write Haiku Poems.

- Decide on the season. Choose one of the seasonal images from the list or write about something you have had experience with and have seen.

- Write the poem as you feel and see it.

- When the poem is expressed the way you like it, then you may choose to follow the syllable pattern and re-write the words.

Haiku Poetry Books

DON'T TELL THE SCARECROW and other Japanese Poems selected and arranged by editors of Lucky Book Club, Scholastic Book Services, 1969

IN A SPRING GARDEN edited by Richard Lewis
The Dial Press, 1965

SIJO

Pronounced (she jo). Sijo poems were written in Korea to be sung. The rhythm was beaten out on a drum accompanied by a lute. A Sijo is unrhymed with six lines. The subject or theme is often nature or the four seasons. There is a syllable pattern. Your Sijo may or may not follow the pattern.

Pattern: Line 1 _____
                    (7 or 8 syllables)
             Line 2 _____
                    (7 or 8 syllables)
             Line 3 _____
                    (7 or 8 syllables)
             Line 4 _____
                    (7 or 8 syllables)
             Line 5 _____
                    (7 or 8 syllables)
             Line 6 _____
                    (7 or 8 syllables)

When you have finished writing a Sijo poem, sing or hum the words while you clap. Is there rhythm in your poem?

This Sijo was written by a sixth grade boy.

I wonder what it's like to

Be a crawling caterpillar.

They're always so alone

And ugly and without friends, and sad...

But when the time comes

Everyone is fooled—a butterfly is born!

Write a Sijo.

- The first sentence will be: "I wonder what it's like to"

- Continue with the poem. _Remember_, this poem is unrhymed.

- When the poem is completed, count syllables if you chose to follow the syllable pattern. Some words can be added or changed.

Do you wonder what it's like to be?

- an insect caught in a spider web.

- a rainbow while the sun is shining.

- an animal in rain without shelter.

- a cloud traveling for miles and miles.

- a crocus pushing up through snow.

- a star thousands and thousands of years old.

- a turtle fighting another turtle.

- a fish caught by a fisherman.

- fog rolling in along the coast.

- a hungry tarantula waiting to eat.

- a toad living at the bottom of a well.

- moss growing on the top of a mountain in winter.

- a snake shedding its skin.

- a cactus that blooms only once every 100 years and then dies.

- an oyster growing a pearl.

- a small fish swallowed by a shark.

- a deer wounded by a bullet.

- a bird that cannot fly. Why?

- a seal resting on a rock in the sun crowded out by other seals.

- a bat living in a dark wet cold cave.

- an ant feeling its way through a tunnel with its feelers.

- a cricket being stepped on by a person.

- a bird flying into a windowpane.

TANKA

Tanka and Haiku poems were first written in Japan. Tanka poems have five unrhymed lines. There is a pattern for the syllables.

Pattern: Line 1 _____
                        (5 syllables)
                Line 2 _____
                        (7 syllables)
                Line 3 _____
                        (5 syllables)
                Line 4 _____
                        (7 syllables)
                Line 5 _____
                        (7 syllables)

The spring rain
Which hangs to the branches
Of the green willow
Looks like pearls
Threaded on a string.
                                Lady Ise

This Tanka was written by a seventh grade student:

Blinking Star

Looking in the sky
I saw a bright falling star
Zooming through the dark
My mistake—it's an airplane
With its blinking lights so bright.
                                Marsha

Write a Tanka: Themes for a Tanka

- Compare a color to a season. In what season do you see the color? Why? How does the color make you feel? How does the season make you feel?

- What is a planet? Why does it *stay* in the sky? What would you compare it to? What if it fell into your room?

- Eagles are the symbol of this country. Why was it chosen as the symbol? What does an eagle look like? How and where does it live? Lead the life of an eagle for one day.

- You are in a space bubble above the earth or on the ocean floor. What do you need to stay alive? How long will you stay there? Why are you there? Do you prefer living in the space bubble to living on earth? Why?

- If you could change the weather, how would you do it? What changes would you make?

Tanka Poetry Books

THE SEASONS OF TIME, Tanka Poetry of Ancient Japan, The Dial Press, 1968

the moment of wonder, a collection of Chinese and Japanese poetry, The Dial Press, NY, 1964

CINQUAIN

Adelaide Crapsey, an American poet, created the first Cinquain verse. It is similar to Haiku. Cinquain has five unrhymed lines. There are several patterns.

Pattern #1 Line 1 _____
       (2 syllables)
     Line 2 _____
       (4 syllables)
     Line 3 _____
       (6 syllables)
     Line 4 _____
       (8 syllables)
     Line 5 _____
       (2 syllables)

Pattern #2 Line 1 _____
       (one word...the subject)
     Line 2 _____
       (two words...describing the subject)
     Line 3 _____
       (three action words)
     Line 4 _____
(four words describing feelings about the subject)
     Line 5 _____
       (one word relating to the subject or
       another word _for_ the subject)

A Cinquain poem by Adelaide Crapsey

November Night

Listen . . .

With faint dry sound,

Like steps of passing ghosts

The leaves, frost-crisp'd, break from the trees

And fall.

Adelaide Crapsey

Write a Cinquain.

- What month is it? Choose this month or a favorite month to write about in your poem. What can you see, feel, hear, touch or smell as you walk outdoors? Follow either pattern for your poem.

The words in Pattern #2 can be written in a shapelike this:

Dog

big, furry

running, jumping, playing

love, companionship, helpful, friend

"Charmin"

Kevin Cedar
4th Grade

Write a Pet Cinquain.

Do you have a pet? Would you like a pet? What kind? Maybe you have a "one-of-a-kind" pet. Describe your pet in a poem. Choose a Cinquain pattern and shape.

Write an "Earth" Cinquain.

Recall any experience you have had with boulders, a waterfall, stream, ocean, lake, glacier, mountain, cave or hill.

Examples:
- swimming in the ocean

- looking for gold in a mountain stream

- climbing over boulders to the top of a mountain

- digging for crabs on a sandy beach

- looking for dinosaur tracks in the foothills

- digging for fossils

- exploring a cave

- walking under a waterfall

Write a Pollution Cinquain.

What problem in ecology or the balance of nature or pollution problem is important to you?

Examples:
> litter
> water pollution
> nuclear waste
> dumping of toxic chemicals
> extinct wildlife
> recycling material

DRAMATIZE A POEM

Poems are written, sung, clapped out, jumped to, used to advertise products and acted out. The poet, Shel Silverstein, writes poems that tell and show action. Two of his poetry books are:

A LIGHT IN THE ATTIC
Harper & Row, 1981

WHERE THE SIDEWALK ENDS
Harper & Row, 1974

Choose one of his poems to act out. Then choose another; and another; and another.

"Orchestra"

"The Farmer and the Queen"

"Me and My Giant"

"True Story"

"Boa Constrictor"

"Snowman"

"The Crocodile's Toothache"

"The Unicorn"

"Peanut-butter Sandwich"

"The Dirtiest Man in the World"

"Spaghetti"

"Put Something In"

"Fancy Dive"

"Bear In There"

"Unscratchable Itch"

"Eight Balloons"

Read other poems. Can you find a poem that would be fun to act-out? Look for action! Let someone read it and you show the action. Or, memorize the poem and say it as you perform.

Act-out verse stories by Dr. Seuss. Start with THE CAT IN THE HAT. Then, act-out SCRAMBLED EGGS SUPER! and HORTON HATCHES THE EGG and HOW THE GRINCH STOLE CHRISTMAS.

POETRY ACTIVITIES

- Attend meetings when a poet is the guest speaker.

- Find a poet in your community through a college or the local library. Ask the poet to speak or give a workshops for your poetry club or to your classroom.

- Find out how poets get their poetry published. How are books printed, illustrated and distributed? The school librarian will guide you in finding the information.

- Read biographies of your favorite poets.

- Ask permission to start a poetry bulletin board. Write and display poems.

- Meet with other children that enjoy reading and writing poetry. Volunteer mothers could meet with you. Give each other ideas and suggestions for writing poems. Read poems aloud. Write group poems.

- Write to a poet. Poets will sometimes answer your letter. Poets like to know which of their poems you <u>especially</u> liked, where you live, how old you are and what you like to do. You might send a poem you have written. This is how you write to your favorite poets:

  > Choose poems you like to read. Who wrote the poems?

  > Look inside the published book of poems for the name of the publishing house. There will be an address in the book. If there is not, ask the librarian to help find the publisher's address.

  > Address the envelope to the poet and send it to the publisher's address or publishing house. *Be sure to write your return address on the envelope.

LISTEN TO THE MUSTN'TS

Listen to the MUSTN'TS, child,
Listen to the DON'TS
Listen to the SHOULDN'TS
The IMPOSSIBLES, the WON'TS
Listen to the NEVER HAVES
Then listen close to me—
Anything can happen, child,
ANYTHING can be.

Shel Silverstein

GLOSSARY

acrostic...letters in one word that are written vertically forming a verse.

adjective...a word that tells about or describes a person, place or thing.

alliteration...repeating the same sound over and over.

chant...words or syllables sung in the same tone.

cinquain...a poem with five unrhymed lines.

clerihew...a biographical quatrain verse.

collage...a poem using different materials and words in a design.

concrete poetry...a poem in which the words form the shape of the subject.

couplet...a stanza with two lines.

diamante or diamite...the words in this poem form the shape of a diamond.

found poetry...words in the poem are found on a variety of printed material.

free verse...poetry that follows no set pattern. It flows freely as the thoughts of the poet flow freely.

haiku...Japanese image poetry with three unrhymed lines.

hyperbole...exaggeration to make a point.

jingle...a short verse with repeated sounds and strong accents on the words.

kenning...old English metaphor using a compound word.

limerick...a five-lined poem with rhyming words.

lyrics...words to a song. The words are a poem.

metaphor...the same idea or object described by using or suggesting a different likeness.

narrative...a poem that tells a story with a beginning, middle and end.

nonsense word...a word that has no special meaning. It is not found in the dictionary.

noun...a person, place, thing or condition.

onomatopoeia...a word or nonsense word that imitates a sound.

parody...a poem that mimics another poem in a humorous way.

patchwork poem...pieces of pictures and words that create a picture poem.

pattern...a model or example.

personification...to think of an object as a person.

poem...a composition using rhythm and sometimes rhyming words in verse.

poet...a person who writes poems.

poetry...the art of composing poems. Putting experience, thoughts and feelings into verse.

quatrain...a stanza with four lines

rhyme...words that sound alike. The words do not have to be spelled alike.

rhythm...movement in a regular accent or beat.

sijo...Korean poetry with six unrhymed lines.

simile...two unlike things are compared by using the words like or as.

stanza...a group of lines forming a section of a poem or song.

syllable...a separate sound made in pronouncing a word.

tanka...Japanese poetry with five unrhymed lines and 31 syllables.

tercet...a stanza with three lines and various rhyming patterns.

tongue twister...repeating the same sound to "twist a tongue."

triangular triplet...verse written in a triangle shape.

verb...an action word that shows doing, being, or happening.

verse...a section of a poem...a single line of poetry or group of lines usually in rhyme.

ACKNOWLEDGEMENTS

Three Simile Comparisons, reprinted from the December 1977 issue of <u>Ranger Rick</u> magazine, with permission from the publisher, the National Wildlife Federation. Copyright © 1977 NWF.

"Who Dat," "I quit!" and "Blinking Star" reprinted with permission from SPARKLING WORDS by Ruth Kearney Carlson.

"November Night" by Adelaide Crapsey reprinted with permission Alfred A. Knopf, Inc. Adelaide Crapsey Foundation from VERSE by Adelaide Crapsey.

"RainPoem" by Elizabeth Coatsworth reprinted with permission of Macmillan Publishing Company from POEMS by Elizabeth Coatsworth. Copyright © 1957 by Macmillan Publishing Company, renewed 1985 by Elizabeth Coatsworth Beston.

"Tag Along" by Nina Payne reprinted with permission of Atheneum Publishers, an imprint of Macmillan Publishing Company, from ALL THE DAY LONG by Nina Payne. Copyright © 1973 by Nina Payne.

"Dragon Smoke" by Lilian Moore, reprinted with permission of Atheneum Publishers, an imprint of Macmillan Publishing Company from I FEEL THE SAME WAY by Lilian Moore Copyright © 1967 by Lilian Moore.

"Who to Pet and Who not to" by X.J. Kennedy from ONE WINTER NIGHT IN AUGUST and other nonsense jingles. Reprinted by permission of Curtis Brown, Ltd. Copyright © 1975 by X.J.Kennedy.

"Hey, Bug!" printed with permission of Atheneum Publishers, an imprint of Macmillan Publishing Company, from I FEEL THE SAME WAY by Lilian Moore. Copyright © 1967 by Lilian Moore.

"Lasagna" by X.J. Kennedy reprinted by permission of Curtis Brown, Ltd. Copyright © 1975, 1977,1978, 1979 by X.J. Kennedy.

"five line poem by Lady Ise" credit line: Kenneth Rexroth, ONE HUNDRED POEMS FROM THE JAPANESE. All rights reserved. Reprinted by permission of New Directions Publishing Corporation.

"Blue Wool Monkey" by Myra Cohn Livingston from WIDE AWAKE AND OTHER POEMS by Myra Cohn Livingston. Copyright © 1959 by Myra Cohn Livingston. Reprinted by permission of Marian Reiner for the author.

"Flowers are fragile" by Debra Jeffers from THE FIRST BOOK OF SHORT VERSE selected by Coralie Howard. Copyright © 1964 by Coralie Howard. Reprinted with permission of the publisher, Franklin Watts.

"Katie's Shadow Poem" by Katie Vinz from FOR KIDS BY KIDS a book of poems and pictures edited by Dan Jaffe and Sylvia Wheeler BK MK Press, Kansas City, MO, 1977.

"Summer Wind" from LET THEM WRITE POETRY by Nina Willis Walter Holt, Rinehart, Winston, Inc.

"The Toad" from IN A SPRING GARDEN edited by Richard Lewis. The Dial Press, NY, 1965.

"An Historic Moment" from PICK ME UP a book of short poems edited by William Cole, The Macmillan Company, 1972.

"M is for MASK" from LAUGHING TIME by William Jay Smith, Delacorte Press/Seymour Lawrence, 1980.

"I" from SOMEBODY TURNED ON A TAP IN THESE KIDS edited by Nancy Larrick, Delacorte Press, 1971.

"Bug in a Jug," "Dandelion" by Hilda Conkling, and "I've Got a Dog" from the RANDOM HOUSE BOOK OF POETRY FOR CHILDREN selected by Jack Prelutsky, Random House,1983.

"Shopping" by Ilo Orleans from MOTHER GOOSE pictures by Tasha Tudor Walck Publishing, 1944 credit to David McKay Co. a division of Random House, Inc.

"Whee" from SEEING THINGS by Robert Froman (Thomas Y. Crowell). Copyright © 1974 by Robert Froman. Reprinted by permission of Harper & Row, Publishers, Inc.

"I wonder what it's like to" from PASS THE POETRY PLEASE by Lee Bennett Hopkins, Citation Press, NY, 1972. Reprinted by permission of Lee Bennett Hopkins.

"Listen to the Mustn'ts" by Shel Silverstein from WHERE THE SIDEWALK ENDS the poems and drawings of Shel Silverstein, Harper & Row, 1974.

"The True Names of the Months of the Year" from AND THE FROG WENT 'BLAH' by Arnold Spilka. Reprinted by permission of Marian Reiner for the author.

ABOUT THE AUTHOR

Sue Thomas graduated from the University of Northern Iowa with a Bachelor of Arts Degree in Elementary Education. She taught first, second and third graders. After co-authoring creative drama books entitled CURTAIN I and CURTAIN II for Trillium Press, Sue presented a series of drama segments on the televised children's program "Hoorah for Kids!" Her creative time is divided between writing poems, activities, stories and books for educational publications.

Copyright © 1993, Royal Fireworks Printing Co, Inc.

All Rights Reserved.

Royal Fireworks Press
First Avenue
Unionville, NY 10988
(914) 726-4444
FAX: (914) 726-3824

Royal Fireworks Press
78 Biddeford Avenue
Downsview, Ontario
M3H 1K4
FAX: (416) 633-3010

ISBN: 0-88092-079-3

Printed in the United States of America by the Royal Fireworks Press of Unionville, New York.